Come to the Water

Sharon Hürkens

Avid Readers Publishing Group

Lakewood, California

Avid Readers Publishing Group

http://www.avidreaderspg.com

ISBN-13: 978-1-61286-302-3

Printed in the United States

Table of Contents

This devotional was written with love for God's life changing power through His Word. As we spend time each day with Him, He works in us and perfects our lives according to His desire. He wants us to walk in that life of fulfillment He has for us. Spend time with Him daily and you will experience Him in a completely different way.

Pastor Sharon Hurkens

www.shedawayministries.com

sharoneastrockaw@aol.com

You will find it necessary to let things go, simply for the reason that they are too heavy. – Corrie Ten Boom, The Hiding Place.

1

Emotional Downloading

"Where is Sarah, your wife?" the visitors asked.
"She's inside the tent," Abraham replied. Then
one of them said, "I will return to you about this
time next year, and your wife, Sarah, will have
a son!" Sarah was listening to this conversation
from the tent. Genesis 18:9-10 NLT

    ALL BREIEVER'S STRUGGLE with
questions regarding their faith at some time or
another in their lifetime. Abraham and Sarah had
doubted that they would be able to be the parents
of a child. (Genesis 18.) Throughout the book
of Psalms, we see David crying out to God often
doubting whether God hears him or not.

The list of heroes goes on and on. The subject of
religious doubt can often be denied, yet many suffer
from it without getting freedom. Religious doubt
is a *lack of certain truth regarding the teachings of
Christianity or one's personal relation to them.*

This can include questions about our personal
assurance of salvation, or the truthfulness of our
beliefs. We may question our pain and suffering
and the reality of unanswered prayers.

Unfortunately, many have false beliefs regarding
the nature of religious doubt, such as:

1

- Doubt is always sinful, perhaps even unpardonable.

- Doubt never occurs to believers.

- Doubt is rare among believers, and the list goes go.

There are at least three distinct types of religious doubt:

Factual doubt which questions the historical or scientific nature of Christianity;

Emotional doubt which is usually related closely to our moods or feelings and often asks "what-if" questions regarding whether our faith could possibly be mistaken.

Volitional doubt usually portrays itself as one's lack of will or desire to follow God completely.

Of these three, I want to address **Emotional doubt** as it is the most common and hurtful. Despite our past or present situation or events, our *feelings* are not actually affected by this, instead it is our *interpretations of these situations or events*. It is how we actually "*download*" information and life changes that cause us to experience **emotional** doubt.

As Christians, our faith is **Correcting our** crucial to us, but if we persist **thinking is the** in thinking or telling ourselves **KEY to peace** how bad life is, or, keep questioning whether or not God's promises to us are true or not after all? painful feelings will result.

An emptiness will fill our hearts. But, on the other hand if we change our words and thinking, and practice *truth,* our feelings will change as well.

Philippians 4:6-9 promises peace in place of our anxiety.

"Don't worry about anything; instead, pray about everything. (*change your format, instead of worrying about the situation, pray)* Tell God what you need, and thank Him for all He has done. Then you will experience God's peace, which exceeds anything we can understand. His peace will guard your hearts and minds as you live in Christ Jesus." And now, dear brothers and sisters, one final thing: Fix your thoughts on what is true, honorable, right, pure, lovely and admirable. Think about things that are excellent and worthy of praise."

Doubt is a difficult subject, but the application of God's truth can and does bring substantial relief. Doubting itself is not a sin, but believing the doubt and giving in to the consequences of believing the lie, can lead us to sinning. Correcting our thinking is the key to peace.

Prayer: Thank you Lord that I can come to you with my doubts, concerns and heaviness of heart. I give you my situation, I lay it at your feet and I ask you to help me walk in your truth. Thank you in advance for undertaking in this situation and thank you for your peace.

Life Application: List the biggest doubt that you have at this time. Lay every burden on this sheet and give it to God. What will change if you knew God hears your cry and will help you in this difficult situation. How will you walk into your day differently?

2

Facing Your Whitespace

You will show me the way of life; Granting me the joy of your presence and the pleasures of living with you forever. Psalm 16:11

LIFE HANDS US different seasons. Being a creative person, I often see objects in light of a different perspective than anyone else may. One of these seasons in life can also be known as "*Whitespace.*" Webster's dictionary explains it in this unique way.

*In page layout, illustration and sculpture, **white space** is often referred to as a negative space. It is the portion of a page left unmarked: White space should not be considered merely 'blank' space — it is an important element of design which enables the objects in it to exist at all; In-expert use of white space, however, can make a page appear incomplete.*

Those who love to paint, write, or sculpt, experience the daunting seasons of white space. However, this experience is not limited to only those who love to fill pages either with words or art. Everyone faces times when "white space" stares directly at them, teasing them with emptiness. Maybe trying even to intimidate and cause feelings of fear and insecurity.

There is nothing more intimidating than facing your days when the future is blank. Your future may **Never fear the emptiness of time that hunts you.** appear blank because of circumstances you find yourself in whether financial, relational or health wise.

If we stare long enough at the emptiness ahead of us, we may experience intimidation, confusion or fear. Yet, if we look at the white space as a gift given to us so that we can pour out our thoughts and plans on to it, we will see it for what it is, a beautiful opportunity to use the space for God's Glory.

An artist does not see the empty page as being negative. No, they see it as an opportunity to fill it with what is given to them by God.

Whatever your spiritual white space is what is staring back at you, begging you to pour out and create beauty with words or art, use it as a testimony to glorify God and His faithfulness to us, His children. If we did not have times where life was offering us the choice to pen words of praise to God through our trials and journeys, how would we be the witness of God's deliverance and perfect plan using us as His instruments to bring Light to this very dark world?

Never fear the emptiness of time that taunts you. You are in Christ and the white spaces you experience are beautiful. It is in these times that you will see God pour out His plan and complete the space.

Prayer: Lord, I see no hope in my future, all looks bleak and empty. I'm staring into the future where I cannot see any fruitfulness or purpose. Please help me once again to see my life as you have created me to be. Direct me Lord that I can once again see my life of purpose. Thank you God.

Life Application: What is your "white space?" What are you not seeing in the days ahead? Write down the empty feelings you have about any of your situations. It may even be that you need to see God's Hand writing on the empty sheet of your children's lives, or that of your spouse.

3

Establishing Your "New Normal."

This means that anyone who belongs to Christ has become a new person. The old is gone; a new life has begun! 2 Corinthians 5:17

I ALWAYS WONDERED how I could describe the next phase of life after a person has experienced situations or traumas and then has had to adapt to life afterwards. I was reading an article the other day about establishing your "new normal" and I got so excited because this is it. This is that phase in life which needed words to describe living after tragedy or any kind of life changing event.

This makes it so much easier to adapt to the changes which take place so that it impacts our lives in a positive way.

Change is something that is to be expected. The way we do "life" in 2016 is different to the way people lived at the turn of the century. Computers and technology has shifted the way we do ministry and business.

Scripture is full of the "new normal." After we accept Christ as our Savior, we start to live a completely different lifestyle to the one we knew before.

This Scripture in 2 Corinthians is Paul's most characteristic expression of what it means to be a Christian. Our identification is now with Him by faith and His death and resurrection for us changes everything. This new existence becomes our normal way of life. The way we did things before we knew Christ, no longer is our "normal." Our relationship with Christ affects every aspect of life.

When Christ comes into our lives there is a re-ordering of how we look at everything in life through Him.

This gives me a sense of hope for the uncertainty of the future. Every decision we as Christians need to make must be based on who we are now in Christ. Not, who we used to be without Christ.

We look at our future with a sense of Hope and a feeling of knowing that we are not without a Savior guiding and

Scripture is full of living life and having a "New Normal"

protecting us all the way. Despite what the world says, they are the ones living the "old way" of life. We have walked away from the past and all it had for us. Our new normal is one full of hope and purpose.

Those walking in the old *normal* will not experience the peace we have of having a Savior who knows about our tomorrows and that in fact He has a purpose for us in that tomorrow.

Live out your life now with knowing that Christ has your life in His Hands. This is your new *normal*.

The old normal was where you were in control of your life.

Prayer: Thank you Jesus that you have my life in Your Hands. Help me to see my life and the world around me through the newness of life that you have given me.

Life Application: Your old normal versus your New Normal. How does it look like on paper? Write it down and see how amazing it is. A life of hopelessness (old normal) versus a life filled with hope and a future of purpose (new normal)

4

Is Fulfillment an Emotion?

The thief's purpose is to steal and kill and destroy. My purpose is to give them a rich and satisfying life. John 10:10

GOD HAS GIVEN US Christ and He came so that we may have a life that is satisfying.

I have given this life of fulfillment a lot of thought. What exactly does being fulfilled mean? Is it a feeling? Are we to walk around with this warm fuzzy feeling inside all the time or else we are not walking the walk? What about the reality of life such as when the heat won't work and it is 9 degrees Fahrenheit outside? Or we do not have enough money to pay the bills? When the doctors give us a bad report back from medical tests done?

Do we act like ostriches and stick our heads in the sand forgetting that the rest of our body is sticking out for the enemy to tear us apart? No! The beautiful promise of fulfillment *is* that peace, which Jesus speaks about surpassing all understanding even when the heat won't work, or the money won't stretch to cover the expenses and the doctor's report is frightening.

Our world is not perfect and listening to the news makes you want to run to the store and stock up on non-perishables because the end is in sight or our circumstances are dim, this *is* when we look to Christ for that strength and wisdom to endure.

Knowing Christ and the fact that we can and must come boldly before Him presenting our situation to Him, it is then by Faith that we receive His peace which is the sense of fulfillment. We are seldom able to change our outside circumstances, but it is the inner man where the Holy Spirit can and does bring us to the place of fulfillment. Then by faith (receive, believe and act) we know that God is in control and will guide us through whatever it is where we need His assistance and direction.

The dictionary states that fulfilled *is* a sense of completion. Once we have given our oppressive situations over to God, He then gives us that feeling of completeness. In Christ we are complete.

To answer the question of whether or not Fulfillment is an empty emotion or not, we can see from the above discussion, that the sense of fulfillment that Scripture speaks of which Christ gives *We are seldom able to change our outside circumstances,* us, is not just an empty emotion. It is an active sense of completion. We are complete in Him.

Encourage one another with this promise, that in Christ we are complete. Circumstances and people change, but God never changes, He will always hear your cry. His peace comes to you after you hand over your situation over to Him.

Prayer: Father, please take my life, my circumstances which seem out of control right now and in return give me your life of fulfillment and satisfaction. Help me to walk each day in that knowledge that you came so that I can have a life which is satisfying. Thank you Lord.

Life Application: What does it mean to you when you read this Scripture and it says that Christ came so that you can have a satisfying life? Does it mean a life without trouble? No, of course not! But it means...?

5

Limitless Living

Am I a God who is only close at hand?" says the Lord. "No, I am far away at the same time. Can anyone hide from me in a secret place? Am I not everywhere in all the heavens and earth?" says the Lord. Jeremiah 23:23-24

I NEVER REALLY give any thought to how God is omnipresent, in other words, everywhere. Nor do I think about God and how He transcends time and space. It has just been a fact that I have accepted and never questioned. However, we live in a physical world with its four known space-time dimensions of length, width, height or depth and time. This knowledge that we focus on being a part of the physical world is what limits us and God's work through us.

God dwells in a different dimension – beyond the perception of our physical senses. He is not limited by the physical laws and dimensions that govern our world or govern us.

In this Scripture God makes reference to Himself as filling heaven and earth. He is everywhere. This excites me and inspires me to be more confident in my God who transcends space and time. Take this to heart and let it sit deep in your soul till it bubbles out increasing your fruitfulness for God.

It doesn't matter where in the world we are, God is with us. This has especially become a reality to me because of living so far apart from my family and friends in South Africa yet what concerns them, concerns me and God in turn sees and hears my prayers for them. I cannot be everywhere, but God once again surpasses the distance.

I was busy doing chores the other day when I got news that my mom was stressing over family issues. My response was a deep sense of helplessness and sadness. I felt like sitting down and throwing my hands in the air, because I could not help her through what she was going through. Suddenly, quietly in my heart I heard what I knew was God's voice, "call her and pray with her over the phone." I did just that. The result was a complete transformation in her outlook, her attitude and she was able to go on with her life knowing God enables us to walk confidently through our situations because He is in control if we give it over to Him.

Why am I even sharing this with you, you might ask? Well, you also experience times where you are limited to act on someone's behalf such as a family member or friend. But God is not limited and He wants to work through us so that He can be glorified.

As believers, we have a deep sense of comfort knowing that God, though timeless and eternal, is in time with us right now; He is not unreachably transcendent, but right here in this moment with us. And because

My God transcends space and time.

He's in this moment, He can respond to our needs and prayers.

We can experience "Limitless Living" because of Christ. Go ahead and live like there are no limits. Be fruitful in all you do, experiencing a God who has no limits.

Prayer: Thank You God that you are not limited by the barriers of space and time. You oh God are never far away and we cannot hide from You. I do not want to hide from you oh God, instead give me insight to your vastness and of who you are.

Life Application: Knowing that God transcends space and time, how are you going to change your thinking today?

6

Little bite at a Time

*But I will not drive them out in a single year,
because the land would become desolate and
the wild animals would multiply and threaten
you. I will drive them out a little at a time until
your population has increased enough to take
possession of the land. Exodus 23:29-30*

MY NATURE IS SOMETHING which I am at war with all the time. In my flesh, I want to accomplish huge tasks all at once. Unfortunately, there are very few tasks which can be accomplished all in one sitting. Scripture has so much to say about accomplishing what God plans for us to do, but there are times when it can only be accomplished little by little.

I love the quote: "How do you eat an elephant?"
"One bite at a time."

An elephant is a huge animal. Its skin is tough. To even begin crunching on it, your teeth must be sharpened.

Exodus 23:29-30 explains clearly why often times God does not enable us to rush at something and finish it quickly. In the entire process, the process of waiting or moving forward is not intended to be rushed.

God tells the Israelites that they will not inherit the land before He has driven the enemy out. But He will drive them out "little by little." Why? So that the land and the cities will not be left to ruin and the Israelites will be able to inherit the land in good condition. God also wanted their dependence to be on Him and not on their own ability.

Many times we get frustrated because our plans are not moving ahead as quickly as we think they should. This is the wonderful *If an elephant needs to be eaten, how will we do it? "Little by Little."* reality about God. He knows everything. He has the perfect timing for everything. It is in this truth that you and I must rest! If the tasks seem too large to complete all at once, it is advisable to work at them little by little. Why? Because it is in the waiting and working period that we grow. We see God's amazing hand at work helping us accomplish what at first seems impossible.

God does not overwhelm us with too much at once or too much too fast. Rather, as we can handle things, He does for us, "little by little," exactly what we need. In your "To Do" List for your life, make sure that you trust God firstly with the details of it. When you begin to fret, turn to God and trust Him to go before you and work everything out. The Key is though that you must follow His plan for your life and not your own plan.

Just as God wanted Moses and His children throughout history to be aware of the fact that His Hand was guiding, even when unseen, so He wants us to know that He is guiding our path, even though unseen. God fights our battles for us. In this portion of Scripture God have some secret weapons He would use if necessary and those are "hornets!" Not a nice weapon at all, but an unexpected and effective one.

Place your life's plan in God's Hands; let Him direct your path, *Little by Little.*

Prayer: Lord, You created me and gave me the personality and gifts which I have so that I can accomplish your purpose for my life. Help me to reach your goals for my life "Little by Little." Whatever task it is Lord, whether large or small, let me move forward and not stand stagnant. Thank you Lord that you do not give us too much to handle.

Life Application: What is it that you feel you need to accomplish for God, yet it seems too big to attain? Write it down and then ask God to help you break it down in little steps.

7

Fresh Manna for the Day

*God, your God has blessed you in everything
you have done. He has watched your every step
through this great wilderness. During these forty
years, the Lord your God has been with you, and
you have lacked nothing."*
Deuteronomy 2:7

GOD WAS FAITHFUL to the Israelites
even in their wilderness wanderings. He provided
well for them in the way of food, and water. He
healed their diseases, protected them from whatever
dangers were lurking in the desert and the clothes
they wore did not even wear out. They lacked
nothing, even in the wilderness.

If you reflect on your life and your times of wandering
in the wilderness which means either when you
were in the world and not a Christ follower, or,
when you were experiencing a very difficult season
in your life and you felt as if you were in a *dry* place
there you will see how God had His hand on your
life, providing, guiding and caring for you.

God focuses on bringing us to maturity. He will not
allow us to skip any of the steps in the process and
will make sure we complete it. God calls you and I
to pursue Him with all our strength.

God makes promises and keeps them. We cannot always say that about man. Our trust must not be in our government officials or politicians; they are mere men and women. Our trust must be in God.

Just as He provided for the Israelites fresh manna (bread) every single day, so too will He provide you and I with strength and spiritual food for each day as we spend time reading His word and praying.

Fresh manna, just for today.

Here are two things you can do to get you get through those seasons in life where you may be experiencing a wilderness lifestyle, one that is dry and without hope

Firstly, get on your knees and you cry out to God, *Fresh Manna,* bringing Him everything *just for Today!* you are experiencing, your doubts, fears, anger, etc and then?

Secondly, Read His Word. Every single day, open up the bible. Even if you read a Psalm a day, maybe even read a particular one over again until it sinks in to your heart.

This will give you what you need; this will be your Fresh Manna daily. Don't think about manna or food for tomorrow, God will provide His encouragement and take care of your needs, tomorrow.

Prayer: Jesus, I am experiencing this very dry period in my life. My heart seems cold and hopeless. Today I am bringing you all my cares, my needs, concerns and dreams. I lay them at the foot of the cross and wait for you to provide my fresh encounter.

Life Application: How do you trust God for your fresh encounter with Him today?

8

Out of the Barren Ground

*My servant grew up in the Lord's presence
like a tender green shoot, like a root in dry
ground. There was nothing beautiful or
majestic about his appearance, nothing to
attract us to him. Isaiah 53:2*

WINTER COMES AROUND without
fail, each year. Spring and Summer disappear. The
ground is hard and frost kills off any living plants.
We do not try to plant anything during this season
because it will not survive.

Herod tried to kill Jesus but never succeeded.
The impact that Jesus had during his life, death
and Resurrection has given us the Hope we so
desperately need.

Isaiah spoke of the humble circumstances of
Christ's birth, His growth and development. Despite
the harsh circumstances surrounding the birth of
Christ, He sprang up and continues to thrive even
in the hardest and driest of soils.

Jesus never finds the human heart to be fertile soil.
We are characterized by darkness, greed, envy
and pride. I think of Augustine, whose heart was
consumed with hedonism and how his heart was
hardened and indifferent to the faith of his praying
mother. Then there was Saul of Tarsus, the great

persecutor of the early church, yet his hard and callous heart was softened and became a seedbed for the gospel.

This encourages me when I know someone who seems to be far too hardened against the Gospel and the love that Christ offers them.

No circumstance, no matter how hopeless, is beyond the reach of Christ.

Our culture seems barren and dry yet Christ still manages to take root and thrive in the dry soil of an ungodly culture.

We look around at our place of Ministry and Service. There are definitely areas where the soil is unusually hard and dry. The resistance to the gospel is strong and often met with hostility. Yet in God's time, His seed sprouts. Take China for example enslaved for decades by oppressive Marxism during the twentieth century. Doors began to open and it became obvious that the living Christ is flourishing there.

This is the message of Christ; no circumstance, no matter how hopeless, is beyond the reach of the One who takes root in the most barren place imaginable. Never give up sharing the Hope and Light of Christ to those around you in your workplace or home. Expect Him to do what only He can do and His grace will cover even the hardest heart.

Prayer: Thank you Jesus that you alone are the one who softens people's hearts. Lives change because you came to give us the ability to change with your help.

Life Application: The barren soil you encounter daily is a great opportunity for God to work through your life to influence and impact those who have the hardest of hearts.   God knows what He wants you to do for Him, just be available.   How can you do that today?

9

Pulling yourself Up by your Bootstraps

In everything we do, we show that we are true ministers of God. We patiently endure troubles and hardships and calamities of every kind. We have been beaten, been put in prison, faced angry mobs, worked to exhaustion, endured sleepless nights, and gone without food. 2 Corinthians 6; 4-5

I HAVE HAD to do this often over the past several weeks. Each time I would have a "spirit of heaviness," I literally picked myself up and moved forward.

I read a joke which was:

A man said to a psychiatrist, "I need help. I keep thinking I'm a curtain." The doctor said, "Well, pull yourself together."

I enjoyed the picture that this statement painted but then stopped laughing when I realized "Hey, this is a little like most of us." Do we think we are curtains? No, of course not!

We are Christians, equipped in every way to handle the severity of the battle **Hunted down, but never abandoned by God.**

we are in. Yet, we all struggle at times with our circumstances and we give in to the "doubt", "dark days" etc. Whatever label you want to give your difficult situation, we can and will overcome.

We acknowledge that life at times is difficult. Nowhere are we encouraged to bury everything under the rug or in the garden and stay in a world that doesn't exist. Life is tough at times. We realize and accept that.

But... because of who we are in Christ, we are optimistic and the positive is highlighted. Remember we are equipped by the Holy Spirit Himself to cope. WOW!

Being equipped and so powerfully equipped to top it off, we can accomplish the Impossible. We are *ACTIVISTS*.

Paul goes on to say that we are "hunted down, but never abandoned by God. We get knocked down, but we are not destroyed. Through suffering, our bodies continue to share in the death of Jesus so that the life of Jesus may also be seen in our bodies. vv 9-10 NIV

Paul encourages us to be a realist, an optimist and an activist all in one, changing lives one life at a time.

Nowhere in Scripture does it say we are defeated, no, it says we are victorious, we are over comers. We are free, not bound.

Prayer: Thank you Jesus that you have come so that we can pull ourselves up by our bootstraps. We can walk with our heads held high; we overcome any obstacles in our lives because of who we are in you.

Life Application: There are days when you feel defeated and want to quit. How are you going to change your thinking and attitude when you feel like this again? Knowing who you are in Christ, how can you use this truth from God's Word to apply to your situation?

10

Refuse to Lose

*Elisha picked up Elijah's cloak which had fallen
when he was taken up. Then Elisha returned
to the bank of the Jordan River. He struck the
water with Elijah's cloak and cried out. "Where
is the Lord, the God of Elijah?" Then the river
divided, and Elisha went across. (2 Kings 2:13-
14)*

2 KINGS DEMONSTRATES a great
principle in the account of Elijah and Elisha. Elisha
refused to do anything that would cause him to lose
his focus.

Notice this principle at work in the life of Elisha.
Elisha pursued what he knew. He refused any other
direction. He knew he had a specific purpose which
was to replace Elijah (1 Kings 19:16.) He knew he
had seen God work when Elijah called for a drought,
defeated the prophets of Baal and called for rain
again. Elisha refused to lose focus. He refused to
think any other way. He expected something to
happen, because God is always about something.
He expected that he could participate because God
delights to use men and women in His work. He
expected that God was at work.

Accomplishing what God places in our hands to do,
takes *focus*. We have to take each day very seriously.
I travel quite a bit and each time I get on the plane I

29

am putting my trust in people who have to take their job very seriously. They have to focus on the

As followers of Christ, we must never be distracted or lose our focus on Christ.

task of flying the plane and getting to their different destinations safely. When the pilot prepares to land the aircraft he or she must remain focused to land safely.

Watching the news can frustrate us to the point where we lose our focus and take our eyes off Christ and look to man to solve our political and worldwide problems.

We have all witnessed the Christians being displaced on a mountain in Iraq without food, water, and hope of being rescued. The persecution of Christians in Iraq is undoubtedly a devastating humanitarian crisis and as more lives are lost at the hands of the Islamic State of Iraq and Syria we stand paralyzed and horrified, as little can be done to help them.

Everyone I come into contact with finds this whole situation frightening, intimidating and even makes some very angry. This situation can make us lose our "focus."

Throughout Scripture we see similar situations where people are in captivity, have life or death struggles and face anger as well.

Whatever we want to achieve in life we have to keep our *focus* or we will never accomplish what God gives us to do.

As followers of Christ we must not allow anything to distract us from our Master. Elisha received what he expected – the assurance that God was still there and would use him after taking Elijah.

God uses the servant who refuses to lose his or her *focus*. If we refuse to lose our focus, pursue what we know, expect God to work, and be ready to use what we receive, God will bring us through and use us beyond our wildest imagination! But… we must refuse to lose *focus!* In the midst of the unexpected difficulties, refuse to lose focus and expect that God is at work even if we do not see His Hand. His plan will be accomplished.

Prayer: Jesus, thank you that you have everything in your Hand, Lord. Thank you that despite what we see on the news and around us, you see the whole situation for what it is and you are at work, even if we can't see it.

Life Application: What is it that you are expecting God to work out in your life? What crisis are you in? How can you use this truth principle from God's Word and apply it to your life?

11

Relax your Fist

Therefore, since we are surrounded by such a huge crowd of witnesses to the life of faith, let us strip off every weight that slows us down, especially the sin that so easily trips us up. And let us run with endurance the race God has set before us. Hebrews 12:1

GOD IS ALWAYS revealing His will for our lives and giving us direction for the path that He has designed for us to walk on. It is us who wants to rather "cling" on to that, in our lives, which holds us back. We have the language of Christianity down pat. We know how to encourage others and have enough faith for their situations to be dissolved by God. Scripture however does not give us tools to only pass on to others. No, it is firstly for us, and then we can pass it on if needed.

A perfect example in my life is this. I spent a week with my parents who are physically not doing well anymore. In fact, it was extremely stressful and took hold of my mind and heart in a way that God would not be glorified. I was trying to straighten the crooked and painful path of their situation, one of age and failing health. The frustrating part is that I could not *make it right* for them. I could not guarantee their safety nor the end of their lives being easy.

Each night I would toss and turn, trying to come up with a solution to their situation. Nothing would come. I cried out to God more than I'm sure He wanted from me. Not giving Him a chance to drop His peace where I needed it most. Finally, when I ran out of words, He was able to speak. This Scripture flew into my mind and I laughed until my stomach hurt. God wanted me to *let go that which was hindering me from moving on and attaining His prize.*

The weight we carry unnecessarily, the important moments of crisis and sorrow which we cannot fix, will prevent God from working not only in the situation which our loved ones are facing, but also **Relax Your Fist. Let God do His work.** in our lives. Each one of us has the responsibility of walking with God as individuals. Why would we need God if someone else could fix our dilemma? Where would we see the miraculous Hand of God working if human beings were the solution?

We become bogged down and ensnared by issues which God wants us to trust Him with. We have much to do for the building of His Kingdom and must do what we can but let Him be closely involved in all we face.

I leave you with this promise from God.

Casting all your care upon Him, for He cares for you. 1 Peter 5:7

Prayer: Jesus forgive me for always trying to "fix" everything in my life and that of my family. Remind me Lord that you care for my family more than I could ever and you will undertake for them as well. Help me to relax my fix, open my hands freely to You so that I can give You my burdens, and then Lord guide me to do that which You want me to do.

Life Application: How can you open your fist and release your burdens, cares, and concerns, to God?

What is in your fist?

12

Slaying your Giants

But you belong to God, my dear children. You have already won a victory over those people, because the Spirit who lives in you is greater than the spirit who lives in the world. 1 John 4:4

DON'T YOU JUST LOVE kids and their enthusiasm and confidence? I once heard a parent telling me of his son who just joined the little league baseball team and hadn't even played his first game but he wanted to sleep in his uniform. Though inexperienced, he believed there was no ball that could get by him.

One of my favorite men in the bible, David was just like that. He was the youngest of his brothers, the shepherd with a few sheep, yet he was called a man after God's own heart. Against all odds, David had faith even to face a giant.

David saw the Israelites standing opposite to the Philistines with a dried up riverbank between. Goliath, about 9 feet 9 inches tall was challenging them to send a champion to fight him. This seemed like an impossible situation, in reality it was. But with God on David's side, and David's faith in God's strength, the Giant never saw sunset ever again. David slew him that day.

35

How did he accomplish this? By having *simple* faith! There was never a thought in David's mind that this Philistine wouldn't be defeated. He practiced a *living faith*. A Living Faith is not only experienced at church. Faith is trusting in God through life's circumstances and difficulties. God also gives us the ability to stand when no one else will during a moment of crisis. When we've reached the end of our human abilities, we come to the Lord asking for His strength.

What giants are you facing in your life which you need to slay right now? A financial giant? A hurting relationship? An addiction? A bad report from the doctor? Whatever it is, learn from David's example.

Your encouragement cannot come from the de-feated. As David faced the Philistines, he saw the Israelites **You have already won a victory. How? Through God's Spirit who lives in You.** were afraid, and that they were of no help. He had to look to God who was his source of strength and victory.

David remembered his past victories. We need to remember times when God has answered our prayers, when He has pulled us from hard situations and provided.

David did not trust someone else's army. Someone else's strategy may not work for you. Saul tried to give David his armor. It wouldn't work. God wants to take your history, your abilities and your talents and add His power to accomplish His purposes.

The threats of the enemy are just threats. God granted David victory in the face of the enemy's mockery! Why? Because…"Greater is He that is in you than he that is in the world"

We can be the people after God's heart through simple, living faith. A faith that does not fail in times of crisis. We must remember that our victories we experienced in the past have been through trusting in God. Despite our circumstances or obstacles, God will help us overcome whatever Giant you need to slay.

Prayer: Jesus I cannot thank you enough that because of you and what You did at Calvary, I can overcome my obstacles, any obstacle. I do not have to live defeated.

Life Application: What is holding you back from using your abilities and your talents with God's help to accomplish His purpose for your life?

13

So Little, Yet So Much!

*"There's a young boy here with five barley loaves
and two fish.
But what good is that with this huge crowd?"
John 6:9*

EVER HAD DAYS when you saw the needs around you, yet you realized you have so little to give? I have these days often. It's not even the physical needs as much as the spiritual needs that I see which overwhelms me.

This portion in Scripture has always blessed me and when I saw it three times during my morning in different readings, I knew that God wanted me to encourage others to focus on this portion. He wants us to bring Him our little, whatever that is. If it is finances, gifts and talents, however meagre, bring them to Him and He will multiply it so much so that there will be fruit left over for anyone who may still enter your day.

He said this to stretch Philip's faith. He already knew what he was going to do.
Philip answered; *He was testing Philip, for He already knew what He was going to do. Philip replied, "Even if we worked for months, we wouldn't have enough money to feed them!" John 6:6-7*

It's so cool to see that Jesus did not turn the young boy away because of his *little* that he had to bring to Jesus. Kids usually don't think further than "You need my lunch? Here!" Adults on the other hand will check around them and think "there is no way my lunch will even feed two people, I will just keep quiet, and surely they will come up with a big plan." This is where we are wrong. God is still a God of the miraculous. Nothing is impossible with Him.

He is challenging us today to look at whatever it is we have to give Him. Do you have a teaching ability? The

God wants us to bring Him our "little."

ability to encourage, the know-how of computers and technology? Well, Jesus is saying to you today: "Bring me whatever you have and see how much I do with it."

Prayer: Jesus, I bring to you my talents, my gifts and any other abilities I have. Please Lord, work through me to accomplish your purposes in my life.

Life Application: What do you feel you have that God can use for His Kingdom? What is the little you have that you believe God wants to do the miraculous with?

14

When the path is cloudy

*For we are God's masterpiece. He has created
us anew in Christ Jesus, so we can do the good
things He planned for us long ago. Ephesians
2:10*

WHEN STEPHAN AND I were younger
and we first went into the ministry, in 1984, neither
of us hesitated to jump at any opportunity offered
to us in the local church. We were prepared to pack
up in a heartbeat and go wherever God wanted us
to go. Then, the call to leave our families, sell all
we had, get on a plane to a place we had never
been to before came. At first we were excited at
this completely different adventure. Then reality
sunk in when we started to sell everything and had
nowhere to go and call *home.* Saying goodbye to
those we loved and trusted was very difficult, but
we knew that this was what God had asked us to do.
We needed to cut our ties with whatever was secure
and trust Him when we could not see beyond the
plane ride.

God has always come through for us when we
needed Him to. Was it always clear cut and the
plan easy to see? Rarely! We just had to move
forward and trust that He, who created us in Christ
Jesus to do the good work which He had in mind
for us, would be there when we did not know which
step to take next.

It reminds me of a building being constructed which I saw not too long ago. Some of the walls were going up, but in the middle of the building, with nothing attached to it was a staircase, this huge staircase just going up and attaching to nothing at all. I could not help but question the architect, the men working on the building and the whole design. What on earth was this staircase doing in the middle of nowhere and how were they going to connect it to the rest of the building without messing up the exact specifications.

Needless to say, the building went up beautifully and the staircase was connected just at the right places. The architect knew what he had planned exactly to the finest little detail.

God, too, knows each one of us so intimately that He knows exactly where and when He wants us to walk. The road is long and cloudy, but it is then that we trust His voice and walk towards Him. Whatever our tomorrows hold, He knows about them and if we trust our path to His direction, we will accomplish the great plan He has for us.

I may not know what my tomorrows look like, but God almighty does and in that I trust.

I pray that you will trust Him with your tomorrows, rest in His omniscience and you will learn the peace that only He can give you.

Be strong and of good courage, do not be afraid, or discouraged. For the Lord your God is with you wherever you go. Joshua 1:9

Prayer: Thank you Jesus that my life is in Your Hands. You have a plan and purpose for me and even though I cannot see what my next step looks like, I know you do.

Life Application: Give your future into God's Hands today. Ask Him to direct your path and guide you in all the decisions you have to make. Give Him your day.

15

Where is your Victory?

*"What do you mean, 'If I can?' Jesus asked.
"Anything is possible if a person believes." Mark
9:23*

MANY OF US, have the bad habit of
anxiety, worry, or a fretful heart. I'm calling it
a habit, because most of the time what we worry
about never materializes.

The story in today's scripture tells of a man who
was in the grips of an anxiety attack, his son was in
crisis. Our greatest worries are often over those we
love the most. While worry may sometimes drive
us to the Lord, it can dominate our prayers and we
have trouble claiming God's answers by faith.

From the opening Scripture we see a father whose
son has a health problem which seems to be so
complex that the boy's life was hopeless. The boy's
disease was fitful, mysterious and terribly violent.
We sometimes forget that the Lord delights to work
with the impossible situations.

The man responded tearfully to Jesus *"Help my
unbelief."* His words of doubt revealed that he had
little faith. Have you ever thought about how many
times we have just enough faith to realize how weak
our belief really is? If we can admit that our faith is
weak, we have a place to start. God has a foothold

in our hearts. Worry and anxiety is tantamount to unbelief and unbelief is a great sin.

Unbelief kept the children of Israel out of the Promised Land for 40 years. Unbelief, doubts that God is omnipotent. It doubts the value of all biblical promises and the very truth of Scripture.

Chronic anxiety represents the sin of unbelief, a serious sin which needs repentance. Jesus will help us if we repent of our sin **Unbelief kept the** of anxiety, worry **children of Israel out** and unbelief. If **of the Promised Land** you're worried **for 40 years**. about anything today, come to Jesus with it. Come with your little faith, for He can help you as no one else can.

Where is our victory? It is in admitting our unbelief and asking God to help us in our weakness.

Prayer: Jesus, Help me in my unbelief. Father reveal to me the areas in my life where I need to yield to You more and where I need to trust You more.

Life Application: What are the areas in your life where you are not trusting God with? How are you going to trust God more?

16

Who Holds my Future?

Then the Lord told him, "I have certainly seen the oppression of my people in Egypt. I have heard their cries of distress because of their harsh slave drivers. Yes, I am aware of their suffering. So I have come down to rescue them from the power of the Egyptians and lead them out of Egypt into their own fertile and spacious land It is a land flowing with milk and honey... Exodus 3:7-8

IF WE FOCUS ON Politics and world economics and see the collapse of world economic systems and the constant threat of global terrorism coming to our neighborhoods, we realize that tomorrow is very uncertain. Growing up in South Africa before the change in government, terrorism was an everyday occurrence. Even today, people are still getting savagely slaughtered just because they own property. We emigrated in 1988 when terrorism attacks in the United States were not even thought of yet.

The most sacred concepts of safety and decency are violated as the world becomes more unpredictable and uncertain.

Moses was presented with the same dilemma. His life was safe and predictable. He was happily married to Zipporah and felt secure in his everyday life. Then, God intervened in Exodus 3. Moses was tending his livestock, *there the angel of the Lord appeared to him in a blazing fire from the middle of a bush. (vs. 2)* Curiosity got the better of him and he moved over to see this strange sight – the bush did not burn up.

What do you think went through Moses' mind? He must have been ecstatic. Then he heard the Lord's next statement. *"Now go, for I am sending you to Pharaoh. You must lead my people Israel out of Egypt." (vs. 10)* Suddenly his tomorrow was uncertain.

Moses tried to argue with God,

Who am I that to appear before Pharoah? Who am I to lead the people of Israel out of Egypt?" (vs. 11)

God answered. "I will be with you." (vs. 12)

Nothing has changed. Life is uncertain. One minute you are coasting along with the wind in your hair and BAM! It changes. But... God is still the same today as He was back with Moses. Moses could face the uncertain future because he was assured that God was with him.

The Lord says through the author of Hebrews: *"I will never fail you. I will never abandon you." (Hebrews 13:5)*

And we confidently say *"The Lord is for me, so I will have no fear. What can mere people do to me" (Psalm 118:6)*

We can face an uncertain tomorrow because God is never surprised by what happens during our journey. He is our strength and our Redeemer.

Prayer: Jesus we cannot thank you enough for being our Redeemer. We may not have been *We can face an uncertain future, because nothing catches God off guard.* rescued from Egypt, but you have certainly rescued us from death and despair. Help me today to walk in the confidence that you are with me, no matter what. Thank You for that.

Life Application: From what has God rescued you?

17

The Impossible Task

So the king asked me, "Why are you looking so sad? You don't look sick to me. You must be deeply troubled." Nehemiah 2:2

WE, AS CHRISTIANS are always about building God's Kingdom. We are always looking at ways to encourage, strengthen and obey His call on our lives. God's plan for us is huge. When we actually "take stock" of the vineyard, we are daunted by the task ahead. This is exactly how God wants it. Why? Because then we will rely on Him and not on building our own Kingdom.

Looking at Nehemiah 2 we see him going before the King with a heavy heart.

And I said to the King, "If it pleases the king, and if your servant has found favor in your sight, I ask that you send me to Judah, to the city of my fathers' tombs, that I may rebuild it."

As Nehemiah leaves to go to Judah and rebuild the City, I'm sure he had thoughts of doubt cross his mind that he will not be able to accomplish this huge task. Certainly he faced the same battles we do when faced with the seemingly impossible tasks ahead of us. There are thoughts of doubt, fear, impatience, etc. He battled with the mission; he was concerned about the impossibility of the task, the timetable, cost, and the list is endless. He also battled with those under his leadership and most of all, the enemy.

As we face our daily tasks or the opposition to us accomplishing God's plans in our lives which seem impossible, we need to remember an **God is faithful, no matter what. Trust Him with your impossible situation.** important principle, as did Nehemiah. We must never forget who God is in comparison to our situation. Never forget God's faithfulness in your life.

In verse 17 and 18 we see that Nehemiah reported the tragedy, but he quickly informed the leaders how God had made Him successful up to that point.

But now I said to them, "You know very well what trouble we are in. Jerusalem lies in ruins, and its gates have been destroyed by fire. Let us rebuild the wall of Jerusalem and end this disgrace!" Then I told them about how the gracious hand of God had been on me... Nehemiah 2:17,18

My husband and I always remind one another of the faithfulness of God whenever we are faced with the seemingly "Impossible" tasks. Will there be sickness? Yes. Will our families do things we wish they wouldn't? Of course. But we look back and remember the good hand of God on our lives and we gladly move forward in faith.

It has been our experience that God never gives His people tasks they can fulfill without Him. We must realize that we are there to glorify the Lord in such incredible ways that we don't believe they are possible. We will encounter hostility, we will battle seasons of defeat and doubt, but God will prevail and He will be glorified through our lives.

Prayer: Thank You Lord for never leaving us to do the impossible tasks without your help. You, O Lord have been faithful to us throughout our lives and we give you praise.

Life Application: What impossible situation is looming ahead of you? Bring it to Jesus, He will help you. He's just waiting to be asked.

18

The Shepherds had a new Vision

They hurried to the village and found Mary and Joseph. And there was the baby, lying in the manger.
After seeing Him, the shepherds told everyone what had happened and what the angel had said to them about this child. Luke 2:16-17

YEARLY, WE SPEND SEVERAL weeks looking at what the birth of Christ means to us. After Christmas we get to stand at the brink of a new year, Christmas has come and gone yet fresh in our minds we still have this reality of our Redeemer being born.

When the angel of the Lord appeared to the Shepherds they were *"filled with fear"* And the angel reassured them, *"Don't be afraid!" he said, "I bring yu good news that will bring great joy to all people."* (I just love that, *for all the people*, not some, all.) Scripture goes on to record in Luke 2:10.

The great news concerning this child was then proclaimed to all. When the shepherds walked away having "met" Jesus their lives were changed forever. They had good news to tell everyone. Christ has come to redeem them. You and I who have also "met" Christ have good news to tell everyone. Our lives are changed forever. It does not matter what

51

we did before we met Christ. Once we met Him, we had hope, we had purpose.

Scripture tells us that where there is no prophetic vision the people cast off restraint. (Proverbs 29:18) To cast off restraint means to have no purpose, no hope. One day just rolls in to another and we hear the common phrase "whatever!"

We Christians should not have the attitude or mindset of the "whatever" happening in our lives because of Christ coming to earth and us having met Him. He stands with us today at the beginning of each day, willing to walk with us, communing and directing our paths, changing our lives from the inside out becoming more and more like Him.

What is it that keeps you from smiling ear to ear with this reality? Is it the same fear that the shepherds had that night the angel appeared to *Enjoy being the vessel God created you to be.* them? Remember the angel said to them "fear not." Christ Himself says that to us today. "Don't be afraid"

If you feel as though you have no vision, ask God to help you to see what He has for you. When the Shepherds left Jesus, they walked away with *good news of joy* to proclaim to all. That in itself is a dream we can live. Everyone we come into contact with, we can show the love of Christ. We can pray for them and ask God to open doors of opportunity for us to share the gospel or good news of His redemptive plan for all.

You and I are not like those without a vision, we have so much and so little time. Enjoy being the vessel God created you to be. You are His workmanship, wonderfully and fearfully made.

Prayer: Thank you Jesus that I can wake up to the reality of never being alone again. You are forever with me. Guide me through this day and direct my thoughts and my life.

Life Application: How can the reality that Christ came to earth change your fears and concerns?

19

Unopened Treasures

"I am leaving you with a gift – peace of mind and heart. And the peace I give is a gift the world cannot give. So don't be troubled or afraid." John 14:27

IT IS EXTREMELY FRUSTRATING when we give gifts to someone, whether adults or children and they fail to open them. It is obvious to us who gave them the gift that it is either not something they desire or the price tag is "not right." The gift gets put on the side and forgotten about.

We leave the party with sadness in our spirit because our gift was ignored, yet how often do we undervalue God's immeasurable gifts of grace and peace. We too look for possessions and shallow experiences which the world has to offer.

"Grace" and "peace" are common religious terms that we throw around yet never really unwrap. The "packages" our culture and world offers are opened with excitement and anticipation at what it holds.

However, the gifts given by the world are short lived. When we unpack ***Take a deep breath; relax, because we can live in His peace*** the gift of grace we realize that nothing happens without God's grace. We are alive because of His

54

grace showered on us. We do not have to earn His grace; He freely gives it to us.

As for His gift of peace, I would not want to enter into another day without it. Where can you get that kind of promise from the world? The culture around us is frightening and causes more fear and panic than the empty promises of the politicians or leaders spouting off about "gifts" they can never give us.

Paul had a habit of greeting those to whom he was writing with the assurance of grace and peace reminding them and us today about God's immeasurable gifts to us. We can take a deep breath and relax, because we can live in His peace and grace on a daily basis.

When Paul was in prison and the believers in Philippi were being persecuted, he wrote to them assuring them of God's grace and peace.

Take time today to thank God for His grace given freely to you as well as His peace that He leaves with you. Daily we draw on God's grace and need to rely on His peace to get through circumstances beyond our control.

Don't waste your energy looking for what the world can give, that is so short lived and empty. Instead enjoy the gifts of grace and peace given to you by God for each day. Wait on God expectantly for His direction in your life.

Prayer: Jesus, please give me your peace. I have tried the peace that the world gives me and it is so empty and short lived. I surrender everything to you Lord, all my dreams and goals, take my life and guard my heart and mind with your thoughts and dreams.

Life Application: What is it that keeps you from walking in that state of mind of perfect peace? Could it be that you are looking at your circumstances and seeing how impossible it is to fix? Well, Jesus can help you. But you have to ask. What situations are you in right now that you are trying to fix on your own?

20

Confidence in a King

He was despised and rejected a man of sorrows,
acquainted with deepest grief.
We turned our backs on him and looked the other
way. He was despised, and we did not care.
Isaiah 53:3

AS WE WATCH the news each day, we see the lack of confidence people have in their leadership, whether they are a President, Prime Minister or King.

Most Kings, are not confident in who they are. Oftentimes, they inherited their positions. Some Kings have no vision and countries literally flounder around, with no direction. Some Kings however are groomed from a young age to be brutal, uncaring and murderous.

Jesus knew exactly who He was. He knew He was the Messiah spoken of by the Old Testament Scriptures. Jesus changed His performance that day. Usually His whole life and ministry was one of shying away from publicity. He never dominated or was power-oriented as other contemporary leaders were. But, this day was different. He knew that His triumphant entry into Jerusalem was designed to seal His death. This would stir the anger and arouse the jealousy of the religious establishment to frenzy, setting the stage for the greatest event in all human history.

Not only did Christ know who He was when he entered Jerusalem, but He knows who He is as He enters your life. Jesus comes with a compassion for souls and bodies. Hours after His triumphal entry into Jerusalem, He wept for her. Have you ever seen a king weep for his people?

Jesus was different; He stopped and wept for Jerusalem. He said, *"O Jerusalem, Jerusalem, the city that kills the prophets and stones God's messengers! How often I have wanted to gather your children together as a hen protects her chicks beneath her wings. But you wouldn't let me." Matthew 23:37.*

Jesus healed the broken and gave sight to the blind. Everyone confidently approached Him and He heard their pleas. Jesus healed the people with broken bodies and shattered dreams, the people bruised and despised, those hurt in their souls where no one can see their pain, these He took to Himself and healed them. He *Jesus, unlike any* did it back then and He *king, knew who He* continues to do it today. *was and His role* This is the Jesus who is *in life.* our King.

If you have not already experienced His trans-forming power of His Holy Spirit in your life and in your pain, He wants to touch you and make you whole.

Jesus doesn't give campaign speeches as any earthly leader does. He tells us what we need to hear. He tells you and I that we can't succeed in our own strength. He warns us to face up to it now and to come to Him while we can.

Today we sing our Hosannas, Are we with Him or Not?

Prayer: Jesus, thank you that you care about me. Thank You that you care about everyone in the world and you hear our cries. You see our pain and you bring healing when we allow you to. I thank You that you are my God, You are my King.

Life Application: Knowing that Jesus is a King like none other, and that He is Your King if you accept Him as your Savior, how does this change your outlook on your life today?

21

But God

But God is so rich in mercy, and He loved us so much, that even though we were dead because of our sins, He gave us life when He raised Christ from the dead. Ephesians 2:4,5

TWO LITTLE WORDS, But God... oh how powerful they are. Two little words so powerful, they can change our perspective on life.

A beautiful image of the church found in Ephesians is that it is Christ's beloved.

Ephesians 1:23; And the church is His body; it is full and complete by Christ, who fills all things everywhere with himself.

This Scripture identifies the church as the body of Christ. In Ephesians 2:4 we see these eye opening words, "But God" The verse goes on to say that God is so rich in mercy, and He loved us so very much, that even while we were dead because of our sins, He gave us life when He raised Christ from the dead.

My eyes stopped at these two words as they jumped off the page. Everything stops and revolves around these two words "But God."

No circumstance, condition, problem, difficulty or even impossibility is a matter for these simple yet profound words.

When Noah faced the flood all would have been lost, "but God..."

When Abraham stood at the altar ready to sacrifice Isaac, "but God..."

When Moses faced the Red Sea in front and Pharaoh's army behind, "but God..."

When the world was lost and hell-bound, "but God..."

No circumstance is impossible with God when He intervenes.

We would have stayed in our sinful, deprived state, *but God* acted. He demonstrated His rich mercy! Why? Because of His great love for us! In other words, we are His beloved! We are the objects of His great love.

Even when we were dead in our sins, God made us alive together with Christ. This is God's supernatural intervention! Paul tells us that God made us alive, He raised us up.

Yet, at times we tend to see ourselves in all of our shortcomings, failures, sins, habits and mess. Why would God take a sinful people, save them, clean them up, make them brand new and bring them into His family and declare that they are His beloved?

In verse 7 Paul tells us that God did all of this "in order that in the ages to come He might show the surpassing riches of His grace in kindness toward us in Christ Jesus." Or, in other words, God says, "I did this so that you will know who I am and what is in my heart." At the core of His heart is a flawless, unlimited heart of love! This same God who governs the entire universe says -

You, church, are my beloved. Feeling loved yet? I am.

Prayer: Thank You Jesus that you have raised me up. At times when I am slipping into despair, please remind me who I am in you. That I have life and I can live it to its fullest, because of you.

Life Application: Do you feel loved by God, the Creator of the Universe? If not, ask yourself what is stopping you from experiencing His unconditional love.

22

The Dreaded Period of Waiting

But those who trust in the Lord will find new strength. They will soar high on wings like eagles. They will run and not grow weary. They will walk and not faint. Isaiah 40:31

OH THE DREADED times of waiting for the Lord to answer our prayers. Those hours spent praying and pleading with God to undertake for us in difficult situations. *"When, O Lord will you answer our cry?"*

Sound familiar? I don't think there is anyone on this planet that has not experienced frustration during those times when we know God said He will undertake for us, but Oh, the wait.

Psalm 138: 8 *The Lord will work out His plans for my life. For your faithful love, O Lord, endures forever. Don't abandon me, for you made me.*

The Lord is never unprepared. Can you imagine if He would have said in the Garden of Eden: "Oh my, that's right!" You need food, Adam, I'm sorry, but I failed to provide it for you." No, God would not have said nor done that.

Yet we act as if God's not going to provide for our needs. God sees far ahead and knows what we need before we do, and just as He has put us on this earth with a plan, He will give us the necessary tools or will equip us for that plan. God is so patient.

When we say to God we are willing to learn how to wait with a purpose and we are ready to work for Him, yet we delay in doing the required task because we need to be better equipped or we lack strength. Then we would be able to do what He has planned for us.

It is such a contradiction – we beg God for patience, but what we really want **The Lord is never** is that He would grant **unprepared.** us our wishes so that we don't have to wait for it anymore.

The tools God gives us won't make your boss give you the promotion or the right mate to appear on your doorstep, because those are external changes and the Lord wants the internal growth to take place as that moves you closer to Him. That's the only way we will see everything clearly.

The wait to get through and past the difficult time in your life is the hardest kind of wait. Feeling lonely and forsaken in your pain, you will not be able to see or imagine the rainbow at the other end. Waiting for the pain to stop is oftentimes too hard to handle, but God knows that you will overcome the pain and that this waiting period will produce growth and will have purpose. Remember God never makes a mistake.

We've all experienced our own kind of tragedies that have made us ache for relief. The only way out of the pain is straight through it, but the Lord is with you. You can't stop the events that occur in your life such as disappointment in a career; failure of a marriage, the descent into unhealthy relationships or practices; hatred, bitterness, envy, or greed that overtakes you; your own doubt and lack of faith that has hardened your heart and made you turn your back on God.

These kinds of life tragedies have to be faced head-on. Try replacing your pain with a purposeful wait as you search for the guidance, courage and peace you've lost. You cannot whitewash your past, it must be faced. God knows all the gory details of any failures or mistakes you've made. He just needs you to use them now for something better and that is growth toward Him, without that, you'll wait forever.

I will end with 2 Corinthians 4:18. *So we don't look at the troubles we can see now; rather, we fix our gaze on things that cannot be seen. For the things we see now will soon be gone, but the things we cannot see will last forever.*

Prayer: Lord I come to you today; I bring you all my baggage, all my pain. I lay it at your feet, Please Lord give me the rest that only you can give. Thank you Jesus! Help me to keep looking to you so that everything else fades away.

Life Application: What can you bring to the feet of Jesus today? What are your concerns?

23

Promises from God

Trust in the Lord, and do good; Then you will live safely in the land and prosper; Take delight in the Lord, and He will give you your heart's desires. Commit everything you do to the Lord. Trust Him and He will help you. Psalm 37:3-5

DURING THIS PAST week I have had so many conversations with people regarding promises and how often their promises which were made to them seemed to be shaky. There are even times when we believe God has promised us something and just before the promise is fulfilled, the promise looks as if it is going to collapse. Our faith is shaken, and our hope in the promise being fulfilled is lost. This is exactly what Satan would like for you to hang on to, a lost promise. He wants you to have your hope crushed.

There are several examples of people receiving promises from God and their hopes were dashed before the promise was fulfilled. A great example is of course, Abraham **O Lord You alone are my hope. Psalm 71:5** and Sarah. Abraham was promised by God that Sarah would have a son and he would have many descendants. Of course, it didn't happen immediately, so Sarah and Abraham doubted God

66

and made their own plans to try and fulfill God's promise to them. (Genesis 16)

By Abraham and Sarah trying to make God's promise to them a reality quickly, they actually made things worse for everyone. This happens to us as well. It may be that you have been offered a job and you know that it was only God who opened those doors for you. Then suddenly, the job seems to be unsteady and things are not looking so good. This is when you need to hang on to God's promise of providing you with what you needed, a job. There are so many instances which take place in our lives where we need to hang on to God's fulfillment of His promise to us, that I cannot mention it all here.

The Scripture found in Psalm 37 is one of the most popular Scriptures used. It has however a condition in it and that is that you must *trust in the Lord*. Delight yourself in Him, committing your way to Him so that He can bring it to pass.

Hold on to God's faithfulness. See how He has brought you through so many difficult situations already. Make note of how He fulfills His promises to you each and every time.

Prayer: Lord, I am trusting you to fulfill Your promises to me. Help me Lord to do my part in our relationship together. Help me not to lose my Hope in the answer to my prayer. Thank You Lord that you have my life in your hands.

Life Application: What promises do you believe God gave you and you are waiting on them being fulfilled? How can you apply your level of trusting God that He will not let you down?

24

My Head VS My Heart

*If you openly declare that Jesus is Lord and
believe in your heart that God raised him from the
dead, you will be saved. For it is by believing in
your heart that you are made right with God and
it is by openly declaring your faith that you are
saved. Romans 10:9-10*

THIS PORTION OF Scripture is literally
jumping off the page at me saying "*true biblical
faith originates in the heart.*"

Over the past several weeks, God has been hitting
me over the head with different scenarios of people
who are dealing with "the old man" and "the new
man."

There are those Christ followers who have studied
the bible all their life never to be affected or
changed by it. This puzzles me because the Word
of God is alive and life changing. It never leaves
us unchanged.

We are all part of this world and we are definitely
influenced by it. The worldview says,

> ➢ There is no God, all gods are equal;

> ➢ There is no heaven or hell;

- ➢ Love is what you make of it;

- ➢ Give in to the desires of your flesh;

- ➢ Work out your own Religion;

- ➢ Prayer is removed from schools, public places and government;

- ➢ There is no hope for a better life;

- ➢ We cannot experience a life of fulfillment.

And the list goes on. We are very aware of the daily influencers and voices filling our heads.

In the opening Scripture the verb *believe* shows us that the result of the act of belief is righteousness. Lifestyles are changed.

On the other hand, if we just accept the Scriptures with our intellect or minds, we can remain unchanged by it. By accepting truth mentally does not mean we believe or are exercising faith. We need to move from our minds to the seat of the source of life, which is the heart. When we literally receive the word by faith believing from our hearts, there is the miraculous life changing experience or metamorphosis happening.

I don't have enough pages to really focus on the different aspect of our thought life and the actual walk of the truth which is embedded in our hearts.

God wants to encourage us to dig deep within us using the truths we have learnt and established in our hearts to overturn the daily impact the world and its views are feeding our minds. Yes, we are to guard our minds, and there are many scriptures focusing on the mind and its impact on our lives. It's a *matter of the heart* which can help the mind enact on what it knows to be truth.

Prayer: Jesus, help me to believe with all my heart that Your Word is alive and will change me forever as I commit it to my heart and commit to share Your truth with those around me. I confess with my mouth Lord that You are Lord and Savior of my soul. My life Lord is in YOU!

Life Application: What part of the Christian walk do you feel as if you understand it with your mind but it's not a part of your make up? Not coming from your heart.

25

Surrendering Your Doubt

Search me, O God and know my heart; test me and know my anxious thoughts. Psalm 139:23 NIV

HOW DO YOU SURRENDER, believe, accept and follow God's guidance? It isn't always obvious, it is not even complicated, but God's guidance is guaranteed, if we want it.   God, throughout His Word promises us that He will help us, not just on Sundays or when we're ill or when we have life-altering decisions to make, but forever. **Matthew 28:20b says "And be sure of this: I am with you always, even to the end of the age."**

Nowhere in scripture do I read that God discriminates on who you are or your race or age, before He will help you. There are no qualifications needed before He will help you. My bible says "ALWAYS" and there is no double meaning or outdated definition for that word. Why then do we fight the Lord when He wants to guide and help us? Why do we wrestle with Him and lose sleep?

I know, because it goes against our human quest for control. We need to control all that we can. We have trouble with accepting that which **Romans 12:12 says Rejoice in our confident hope. Be patient in trouble and keep on praying.**

71

we cannot see. I've fought the Lord often in my life and doubted His power, time and again. But through each wait, He's helped me get closer to Him so that I don't fight as hard or doubt as much the next time. He is forever patient with my spirit and my stubbornness.

Where do we start when we need to listen for God's guidance, with pain and confusion so heavy on our hearts? Surrendering your doubt to the Lord can seem like an impossible task when so many questions and fears are pressing on your mind.

There is unparalleled joy in the pure surrender of your doubt to your Lord. Focus on the times that you have felt His gentle guiding hand and let those experiences carry you now. You cannot be joyful and doubtful at the same time. Which feeling do you think your Lord wants you to embrace? You can do nothing with a doubt except validate it or eliminate it. It's your choice. Choosing to eliminate it, you can replace it with joyfulness.

The cornerstone of our lessons in life is being faithful in prayer.

Isaiah 42:16 says: I will lead the blind by ways they have not known, along unfamiliar paths I will guide them; I WILL turn the darkness into light before them and make the rough places smooth. These are the things I WILL do; I will NOT forsake them. NIV

Relinquish your control to God today. He does not want you to be so heavy burdened.

Prayer: Jesus, I thank you that I can come to you unashamed because of who I am in you. I bring to you today Lord all my heaviness of heart. All my issues and concerns, I lay them down. Thank you father that you will lead me by ways I have not known; along unfamiliar paths you will guide me.

Life Application: What are some of the worries, concerns, issues and road blocks you are bringing to God today. Be Honest, He sees everything.

26

The Deal

Even though the fig trees have no blossoms, and there are no grapes on the vines; even though the olive crop fails, and the fields lie empty and barren; even though the flocks die in the fields, and the cattle barns are empty, yet I will rejoice in the Lord! I will be joyful in the God of my salvation! Habakkuk 3:17, 18

THERE IS THIS annoying game of "words with Friends" that I sometimes resort to when I need to quiet my mind from the action of the day. There are times when I am *dealt* a good *hand* of letters and the words that I form give me lots of points. Just as there are letters handed to me that enable me to form great words, so are there letters that are absolutely worthless and I lose to my opposing player, but I mean really lose. It's almost embarrassing, that is how so low my scores are. It is at times like these that I want to throw the game away. I would really only like the letters that give me great scores.

Then this Scripture found in Habakkuk comes to my mind and I see how this dumb game can be likened to life. We are not always faced with situations which are easy. In fact, life can be very difficult at times and frustrating, yet, the difficulties find us and we are smack bang in the middle of predicaments, health issues, or money problems. It seems as if we are handed a bad *hand.*

Unlike the game, we are blessed to be created by God with love and purpose. Despite the difficulties we have to face in life, we rejoice in God and it is through Him that we handle the stressors.

The Prophet gives voice to these words and it is so impactful. Even if the fig tree does not bear fruit nor blossom. *Even if we face impossible situations and our circumstances stink.* Even if the olives fail and the fields give no food, we should still rejoice in the Lord.

Habakkuk's joy was in the God of his salvation. It doesn't matter what life hands us, God is the One to whom we go to for direction and help.

You may be experiencing a season where you feel as though everything has been taken from you and life is looking bleak. You may even think God has handed you a bad *hand.*

Take your strength from placing your life in God's hands and let Him pour His peace and strength into your frail being.

The fig tree will blossom again; the fields will once again give food. But in the meantime, find your joy in the One who formed you and rejoice in God. That is the best *deal* ever. It is neither empty nor barren. It bears fruit all the time.

Prayer: Jesus thank you that You are Sovereign. You have our tomorrows in your hands and you know exactly what is going to happen to us.

Whatever circumstances we may find ourselves in Lord, they do not catch you off guard. Help me to find my joy in You and not in my situation. And even though life may be rough, my life and joy is in YOU!

Life Application: Where do you find yourself today regarding your level of joy? Is it only that you experience joy when all is going well? List your struggles to find joy here and then see how your attitude changes when you let God's light shine in.

27

Daily Steps for Trusting God

I wait quietly before God, for my victory comes from Him. He alone is my rock and my salvation, my fortress where I will never be shaken. Psalm 62:1-2

DAILY WE STRUGGLE with issues and know that we need to rely on God more. We ask questions such as "Will you, oh God be faithful to us in the end of life?" David gives us easy steps on applying ourselves to trusting God.

We are to wait silently before God each day. (v1) Spend time daily in silence before God. This means we are not to complain to Him when things don't go the way you think they should. You are to hang on and let God do His work. All this depends on how much you trust the character of God. God is our expectation, not mankind or situations.

Cling to Something that Doesn't Change (v2-6) when things are rapidly changing around you, cling to something or someone that doesn't change. It's like holding on to a bar or a tree when you're in the middle of a severe storm. You have to hang on knowing that the object will not move or change. God is that rock. As things change around you, He remains faithful. Cling to Him because He is the only One you can trust in the middle of the storm.

Storms come I different forms, not only in the form of losing loved ones, friends or family.

Don't be shaken in Your Faith (vv 3-7) you may ask yourself "Has God abandoned me?" Suddenly you may find yourself shaken in your faith like an old shed swaying in the wind. Take time to be silent before the Lord and let Him minister to you.

Trust Him at all times. (v8) Learn to trust God in every issue you face. We trust God when we have confidence in His character to do what He has promised to do. Trust God regardless of what comes to your life.

Pour Out your heart to Him. Hannah is a great example of a woman who poured out her burden in the tabernacle about her wanting a child. God heard her cry. Another great example is the prophet Hezekiah who spread out a threatening letter in the temple. Be purposeful and passionate in prayer.

God can be trusted when we are in any stage of our lives.

Prayer: God I know that you are my rock and fortress. I need to put my trust in you and not in mankind. Take this present storm from me Lord and give me your breath of peace.

Life Application: What are you currently facing where you need God to show you that He is your stabilizing factor?

28

Hope in a Who or What?

Mary was standing outside the tomb crying, and as she wept, she stooped and looked in. She saw two white-robed angels, one sitting at the head and the other at the foot of the place where the body of Jesus had been lying. "Dear woman, why are you crying?" the angels asked her. "Because they have taken away my Lord," she replied, "and I don't know where they have put him." John 20:11-13

WE ALL DEAL WITH broken dreams and broken promises. Those gut wrenching times when our dreams fall apart. We set our goals, our plans, aspirations and expectations, just as we are supposed to do. Suddenly the life you're living isn't the life you dreamed of at all. You never even expected life to turn out the way it did. There are times in our lives where we find ourselves in utter states of despair and darkness. Yes, this is what the world wants us to believe is the only way. The world's way of doing life is placing hope in a "What!"

But... our hope is not in a what. It is in a "WHO!"

Scripture gives us the hope that we all need so those areas of despair and darkness immediately lighten up.

In the opening Scripture we see how it gives us an image of Mary experiencing the pain of realizing her whole world had crashed.

Mary's hope and world was in following Jesus. She watched how He healed people, fed thousands with a piece of fish and two loaves of bread. Jesus even raised the dead. Now? He was gone. And these *beings"* were asking her why she was crying? Why shouldn't she be crying? Someone had stolen the body of Jesus.

Jesus had given her life; she could dream again, she could think good things about life and the future. Now, all that was gone, the cross had seen to that. What was she to do now?

What is hope? Could it be?

> "Oh I hope it doesn't rain."

> "I hope the stock market doesn't crash."

No, this is not the hope that Christ gave us. That is the hope the world offers. Hope is to the spirit what oxygen is to the body. Without it, we die. Maybe not physically, but we become walking beings without reason to live, empty shells constantly living in a world of defeat.

Placing our hope in a "what" will only guarantee empty dreams which fall apart or crush us. The Hope that Christ speaks of is found in a person, the person of Christ. We place our hope in Christ, why? Because His resurrection proves that He is stronger than any circumstance. He overcame the grave, He lives. If you have had your dreams killed, Jesus can bring them back to life. In fact, He can give you new dreams, ones with purpose and prospect.

Your story is not over yet. God can still do great things in your life and through you. God will meet you wherever you need Him to. He met Mary in her dark place; He will do that for you as well.

Placing our hope in a living Christ enables us to live confidently. It's facing the future knowing that God can and will do something good in your life and the life to come.

Being Christians we can boldly and loudly say with the prophet Job

But as for me, I know that my Redeemer lives and He will stand upon the earth at last. And after my body has decayed, yet in my body I will see God! I will see Him for myself. Yes, I will see Him with my own eyes. I am overwhelmed at the thought! Job 19:25-27

Prayer: Jesus, thank you that I have a living Hope and that Hope is found in You. I don't have to hope in the things that the world calls reality. You live and that's why I have Hope.

Life Application: What are some of the things that you want to put your hope in? How does knowing Christ as being Your Hope change your perspective of that empty hope?

Jesus gives us real life, we can dream again, we do have a future.

29

Joy & Peace, no Matter What

I have told you all this so that you may have peace in me. Here on earth you will have many trials and sorrows. But take heart, because I have overcome the world. John 16:33

I READ THIS AMAZING story about a soldier in Iraq during the last war. He wrote home about his experiences, saying: "We got hit by an Improvised Explosive device (IED) today. My brothers-in-arms were walking out to inspect a civilian car when it exploded. They were both blown back about 100 feet or so. The hilarious part is when they got up, they started yelling and laughing. They were praising God and thanking Him that He spared their lives. One of them, a new believer said this about Christ. "Jesus has been the BEST companion over here. He listens to my every prayer and answers me every morning with renewed strength and a clear mind."

It made me think of life as we know it, today. Daily we are in the combat zone of life, faced with satanic IEDs and demonic snipers every day. We can however, have a peace that passes all understanding because of Christ who has overcome the world. We can be confident that He listens to our prayers and does answer us every morning with renewed strength and a clear mind.

The sentence "*In Me You May Have Peace*" is the most powerful phrase in the bible – in Me. This was Paul's theme. He used the phrase "in Christ" about 100 times. This refers to our union with Christ.

The next sentence, "These things I have spoken" gives us the sense of inner peace which grows from trusting His words. The tribulation we will have in this world alerts us to the reality that our inner peace, based on our union with Christ which grows as we trust His words, will be assaulted by the world. We will be misunderstood, insulted, hurt, have heartache and persecution. However, Jesus ends on the promise that we must "be of good cheer, I have overcome the world." He was saying "I've come into the world and am going to lay down my life willingly. The grave cannot hold Me, death cannot keep Me, I have overcome."

Christ can help us overcome our anxieties and make all things work together for good. He is the **In Christ we find our peace, strength and direction for each new day.** great over comer, whatever we face, our Peace is in Him.

Be of good cheer, I (Jesus) have overcome the world. Rejoice, YOU are an over comer because of who you are in Christ.

Prayer: Thank You Jesus, that I can be confident of the reality that in YOU I find my daily strength and peace. I can rejoice each time the devil throws his darts of discouragement or defeat at me, but I buffet them. Remind me Lord when I forget this truth.

Life Application: What are the Improvised Explosive Devices that you avoid on a daily basis? If you make a list of how much God has protected you from and how You have overcome the struggles of the day, your peace will grow. Those areas which you still need to hand over to Him, He is waiting.

30

When Star Trek turns up empty

...We have even greater confidence in the message proclaimed by the prophets. Pay close attention to what they wrote, for their words are like a light shining in a dark place – until the day dawns, and Christ the Morning Star shines in your hearts. 2 Peter 1:19

STAR TREK IS A BIG HYPE. When the movie first came out people were standing in line for as long as 24 hours to get in to see the movie. Our actions are controlled by our expectations. We wait in anticipation for the next big high in our life. "When I win the lotto…"

During the time of Jesus' birth, the wise men were told by the angels to follow the star to find Christ. What would you be expecting when you found the King of the Jews? Were your thoughts "wow, I hope that He smiles at me," or "this must be some beautiful place where He is going to be found in."

The wise men gave us actions we can emulate when we anticipate things of God and His path.

Firstly they were extremely joyful. They then fell on their faces and worshiped God. Finally they offered the very best they had.

So, how can we do this? We can be joyful at what God does in our lives on a daily basis, we can worship God freely and honestly knowing that we go directly into His very presence and we offer God our best. After all was said and done, the wise men left that humble dwelling as transformed people. They would never look at life the same again. After an encounter with Christ, our lives too are transformed and we are never the same again.

In any season of life, we need to look at God in a fresh way, thanking Him for what He did for us. He came to earth and was a part of our culture and related to us. He met us where we were. He does not leave us there however, He encourages us to be more than we ever expected.

The hype of Star Wars can never fulfil the same way the Light of the World, Jesus does. Star Wars does not transform our futures. It does not change us. Only Jesus, the Light of the World does that.

Come, Worship Your King.

Prayer: Thank You Jesus that you are the one who transforms me. I do not have to wait for the next big hype in the movie field or the political arena; You are always there to be my focus.

Life Application: What is the Big Hype in your life that you think can change your circumstances forever? Is it winning the lotto? Is it finding the right spouse? Make your list and then analyze it to see if it really is life changing or temporary.

31

Recycling

Since you have heard about Jesus and have learned the truth that comes from Him, throw off your old sinful nature and your former way of life, which are corrupted by lust and deception. Instead, let the Spirit renew your thoughts and attitudes. Ephesians 4:21-23

GROWING UP ON a small holding in South Africa with a father who loved to build, brings fond memories and a smile to my face when I compare recycling of building materials and making a new home from bits and pieces of the old one to our life in Christ.

As a child I always wanted a new home, new bedding, new clothes and new school supplies, but always got the hand me downs because I was the 4th out of five children and buying new supplies or clothing when the old ones were still around, was not an option.

As the family grew and more space was needed, my dad would just add on a room but use materials from either, buildings he had broken down such as a horse stable which was no longer needed, or a tennis court which was outdated. He would take the bricks from the stable, although chipped and marked permanently with horse manure, and proudly add on to the already sloppy built home.

Recycling today is completely different. Old pieces of brick, paper and wood may be used to make other articles but they are made to look good.

Our life in Christ is also made up of recycled memories, hurts and joys. We come to Christ who wants to bring healing to our lives as well as move us forward in the plan that He has for us in His kingdom. We limit the power of God working through our lives since our *recycled* memories prevent us from putting on the *new* man in Christ as we rather minister and live our lives unchanged by Christ.

Paul tries to get us to accept the reality of being a new creature in Christ; we must acknowledge that we are no longer the same person we were before coming to Christ. We are a new creation.

"Forget all that – it is nothing compared to what I am going to do. For I am about to do something new. See, I have already begun! Do you not see it? I will make a pathway through the wilderness. I will create rivers in the dry wasteland." Isaiah 43:18-19

Christ brings us that newness in life. He restores our old selves to the point where although recycled, our lives show the new creation of Christ. We lay aside everything that prevents us from God's plan. We move in faith, believing Him for total restoration.

God bless you as you live life recycled, but new - because of Christ.

Prayer: Jesus, help me forget that I have all these obstacles in my life which I have already given to you. Help me to live that new life as a person changed by your mercy.

Life Application: What are some of the things in your life that God has recycled and made new? If you list them, you will be so excited to see how God brings about the amazing change. He does it, it is lasting and purposeful.

What people are saying...

Like a breath of fresh air, Come to the Water will refresh anyone's devotional life. Pastor Sharon Hurkens leads the reader through a journey of choosing a deeper faith by getting the readers' attention when pushes a few theological hot buttons such as cynical doubt, who is in charge of the future and how to wade through inevitable change. Sharon's pastoral gifts are put into action as she tenderly reminds us how God helps us assimilate these sensitive yet crucial areas as she provides solid Biblical answers. Instead of allowing the issues to separate and suffocate us from closeness to God, Pastor Sharon invites the reader in to join her in learning through practical application and prayer. Come to the Water will help reveal the stale areas of your Christian walk and draw you closer to your Creator.

Sheryl D. Giesbrecht, Th. D., international speaker and author,

Get Back Up: Trusting God When Life Knocks You Down,

Experiencing God Through His Names

www.FromAshesToBeauty.com

I have known Sharon Hurkens for over 25 years. She is a woman of God. Her devotional insights will be a help to any Christian. It will make you think about your walk with the LORD from a different perspective.

Pastor Larry Mancini.

www.ingramcontent.com/pod-product-compliance
Lightning Source LLC
Chambersburg PA
CBHW021208020426
42331CB00003B/259